LET it SNOW

Gingerbread,
Cinnamon, and
Christmas cookies

The snow gently trickles down,
the lake rests quiet and still,
the forest glitters with joy,
the Christ child is coming soon!

LOVE FOR THE
HOLIDAY SEASON

# TAKE TIME FOR THE THINGS YOU LOVE

# Advent, Advent, a candle burns

*Christmas Angel Landing Site*

O Christmas Tree,
O Christmas Tree

Winter Wonderland

A blanket
of snow

# HOMEMADE COOKIES
*Santa approved!*

*Merry Christmas*
*say it softly ...*

*... and a star*
*begins its journey.*

Every
snowflake is a kiss
on your sweet
cold nose.

Let my
lantern
light the
way

Heavenly Christmas

Christmas-Spiced apple cider!

A CHRISTMAS WREATH MADE FROM FOREST
BRANCHES; IT'S CHRISTMAS SEASON!

Feast of Love

Lights twinkle & Candles flicker

THE MYSTERY OF CHRISTMAS IS THAT
THE SIMPLEST THINGS, NOT THE GREAT AND
EXCEPTIONAL, GIVE OFF THE GREATEST GLOW
OF HAPPINESS.

Treats and presents—
Christmas is in the air!

Christmas
calories
do not
count

# MY WISHES FOR THE NEW YEAR

Happiness

COURAGE

Pleasure

Love

TIME

SERENITY

# Here's to a Good New Year!

*Out with the old,*

# IN WITH THE NEW!

First edition for the United States and Canada published in 2017 by Barron's Educational Series, Inc.

© Copyright 2016 arsEdition GmbH, München—all rights reserved—Original title: *Winter-Wunder-Land*

For best results, colored pencils are recommended.

All inquiries should be addressed to:

Barron's Educational Series, Inc.
250 Wireless Boulevard
Hauppauge, NY 11788
www.barronseduc.com

ISBN: 978-1-4380-1015-1

Design: Jutta Kopf
Illustrations: © Fotolia: awispa, d3images, gollli; Jan Engel
© Getty Images/Thinkstock

Printed in China

9 8 7 6 5 4 3 2 1

Find more best-selling coloring books at
www.barronseduc.com

## PADS OF COLOR

MAGICAL CATS — Pads of Color — ISBN 978-1-4380-0930-8

DREAM *Laugh* Dance — PADS OF COLOR — ISBN 978-1-4380-1013-7

GARDEN DREAMS TO COLOR — PADS OF COLOR — ISBN 978-1-4380-1014-4

ZEN DREAMS — PADS OF COLOR — ISBN 978-1-4380-1030-4

## MINI PADS OF COLOR  •  MAGIC LIGHTS

Candlelight Magic — MAGIC LIGHTS — ISBN 978-1-4380-1060-1

DREAMS OF FLOWERS — Mini Pads of Color — ISBN 978-1-4380-1009-0

MANDALA DELIGHTS — Mini Pads of Color — ISBN 978-1-4380-1010-6

SEA OF FLOWERS — Mini Pads of Color — ISBN 978-1-4380-1012-0

# RELAX, CREATE, AND DREAM WITH COLORING BOOKS AND PADS!